OF MICE AND MEN

John Steinbeck

AUTHORED by D. Dona Le
UPDATED AND REVISED by Elizabeth Weinbloom

COVER DESIGN by Table XI Partners LLC
COVER PHOTO by Olivia Verma and © 2005 GradeSaver, LLC

BOOK DESIGN by Table XI Partners LLC

Published by GradeSaver LLC, www.gradesaver.com

First published in the United States of America by GradeSaver LLC. 2010

GRADESAVER, the GradeSaver logo and the phrase "Getting you the grade since 1999" are registered trademarks of GradeSaver, LLC

ISBN 978-1-60259-243-8

Printed in the United States of America

For other products and additional information please visit
http://www.gradesaver.com

Table of Contents

Table of Contents

Table of Contents

Teaching Guide - About the Author

John Steinbeck was born in 1902 in Salinas, California, and is known for a large body of work, most notably The Grapes of Wrath, East of Eden, and Of Mice and Men. He attended Stanford University, but left the school after six years without earning his bachelor's degree. Steinbeck then moved to New York, where he was employed as a journalist for The American and as a laborer. He later returned to California and worked in the Lake Tahoe region.

During this time, Steinbeck completed his first novel, Cup of Gold, which was published in 1929. He married Carol Henning in 1930, and then published several novels in the 1930s, among them Of Mice and Men (1937). In 1940, Steinbeck won a Pulitzer Prize for The Grapes of Wrath. He and Henning divorced two years later.

He remarried a woman named Gwendolyn Conger, and they had two children together. Steinbeck continued to write prolifically, publishing a number of novels and short story collections, and was involved in a number of film adaptations based on his works. Steinbeck and Conger divorced in 1948.

Steinbeck's third and final marriage was to Elaine Scott. They remained together until his death, caused by heart disease and congestive heart failure in 1968. Before his death, Steinbeck won the Nobel Prize for Literature.

Many of Steinbeck's works reflect themes and locations that he personally experienced. The most notable among these are the Great Depression, the California landscape, and the lives of migrant workers and laborers.

Teaching Guide - Study Objectives

If all of the elements of this lesson plan are employed, students will develop the following powers, skills, and understanding:

1. Reading well: appreciating the achievement of the author by examining and discussing details and overarching themes and considering how the details contribute to the whole novel; enjoying a good book in the company of other readers.

2. Thinking well: using the discussion questions to draw conclusions from textual evidence and to use such evidence to weigh differing interpretations of the novella.

3. Speaking well: developing oral skills through vocabulary development, debate, dramatic readings, and group discussion.

4. Listening well: developing a taste for good grammar and strong diction; evaluating peers' oral presentation skills.

5. Writing well: creating and sustaining an argument, and using evidence to support the argument in essay form.

6. Understanding: seeing how themes of inequality, friendship, the importance of place, dreams, loneliness and fate play out during the Great Depression in California.

Teaching Guide - Introduction to Of Mice and Men

The novella takes place during the Great Depression and is set near where Steinbeck was born in California. Drawing upon Steinbeck's own experiences as a bindlestiff, Of Mice and Men depicts two male migrant ranch workers who share a profound friendship.

The novel centers around George Milton, a socially savvy and intelligent man, and Lennie Small, his mentally handicapped but extremely large, strong companion. George and Lennie dream of a better life for themselves, once they earn enough money as migrant laborers to buy a homestead for themselves. However, they are thwarted by social inequities, lack of understanding, and perhaps even fate.

Of Mice and Men was initially intended to be a play in three acts, as discernible from its spare form and stark dialogue, but Steinbeck's dog destroyed the first manuscript.. In fact, the work was very successfully adapted into a stage play and Hollywood film after its publication.

The title of the book is drawn from a poem by Scottish poet Robert Burns, "To a Mouse, on Turning Up Her Nest with the Plough." The precise reference to this poem is as follows: "The best-laid schemes o' mice and men/Gang aft a-gley."

Key Aspects of Of Mice and Men

Tone

Steinbeck blends very vivid descriptions of the California landscape with accurate dialogue that is filled with slang and colloquialisms. Though the descriptions and imagery are vivid, they are nonetheless simple. The reader obtains a clear sense of the ranch's natural setting, as well as the unique community of male ranch workers.

Of Mice and Men has often been censored in the United States for what opponents cite as offensive and crude language.

Setting

Soledad, California, during the Great Depression

Point of View

Third-person narrative

Character Development

Lennie does not change significantly throughout the novella; he is a kind-hearted and simple-minded man who listens to George. Initially, George aspires to own a homestead with Lennie, but by the end of the novel, he realizes he cannot escape the lonely life of a solitary migrant worker. After meeting George and Lennie and learning of their dreams, Candy gains some hope, but this is shattered by the novella's conclusion. Crooks displays more of his personality and reveals his loneliness when he interacts with Lennie and Candy. Curley remains a foolish, jealous and belligerent man who demonstrates little understanding of others.

Themes

inequality, friendship, the importance of place, loneliness, unfulfilled dreams and fate

- **Inequality**: Social inequalities are apparent through several characters. Candy is not respected by his colleagues because he is too old for manual labor. Crooks, as an African American, is isolated from and treated poorly by the other ranch workers. Even Curley's wife is looked down upon because she is a woman. Lennie is unequal to the rest of the men because of his mental handicap.

- **Unfulfilled dreams**: Most characters in the novella fruitlessly harbor unfulfilled dreams. Clearly, George and Lennie are unable to fulfill their dream of earning enough money to purchase their own ranch and to carve a peaceful lives for themselves. This becomes Candy's unfulfilled dream as well. Curley's wife once dreamed of becoming a Hollywood starlet, but now she is simply married to a surly, belligerent rancher.

- **Friendship**: The friendship between George and Lennie figures prominently in Of Mice and Men. The other characters wonder why George remains tied to someone like Lennie, whose handicap makes him a burden on the smaller man. Their friendship creates suspicion in most of the men, but respect in Slim and wistful jealousy in Candy.

- **Place**: The idea of place is significant, as evidenced by where the novella begins and ends. The spot by the river represents a haven for Lennie and George, as does their dream of owning a home for themselves. Crooks also values his place and is hesitant to allow anyone into it.

- **Loneliness**: Most characters in Of Mice and Men are apparently lonely. For example, Curley's wife is not only a meaningless flirt; she suffers from true loneliness in her loveless marriage. George and Lennie seek to avoid loneliness in their friendship. Crooks is extraordinarily lonely and grasps at the chance to talk to the other men, even though he initially discourages

Lennie and Candy from entering his room.

- **Fate**: Details throughout the novella foreshadow the climactic events that lead to Lennie's unfortunate death and the end of George's dream. The progression to Lennie's manslaughter of Curley's wife seems almost inevitable. Perhaps Lennie's gentle nature and unknowing or uncontrollable strength, manifested in his accidental killings of the mouse and puppy, make it impossible for him to avoid a tragic fate.

Symbols

• Rabbits: the dream cherished by Lennie to retreat someplace where he can enjoy life, often expressed through his simple desire to touch soft objects/animals/fabrics

• light, or lack thereof: foreshadowing positive/negative events and characters

• hands: strength and power (Curley's crushed hand, Lennie's "paws")

• places: significance of one's personal "space" as identity and as hope for future (the fictitious homestead, Crooks's bunk)

• repetition and storytelling: George's repeated description of the dream homestead; where the story begins and ends

Climax

The climax of the story occurs in the last two sections, when Curley's wife is accidentally killed by Lennie. Her body is quickly discovered, and George realizes right away that Lennie is responsible for his death. Lennie is aware enough to retreat to the river, first described in the beginning chapter of the novella. George stalls for time, steals a gun, and goes to meet with Lennie. As Lennie looks away into the distance, at George's prompting, George shoots and kills Lennie so that he will not have to suffer a worse fate at the hands of the ranch workers.

Structure

The structure of Of Mice and Men is tightly woven, never lacking in rapid action and straightforward dialogue, and cyclical. The story begins and ends at the same location, where George tells Lennie to meet him if they encounter any trouble at the ranch. Each section or "scene" features a self-contained event, which—taken together—provide details that provide the inertia toward the seemingly inevitable climax.

Teaching Guide - Relationship with Other Books

• Compare with Steinbeck's most famous work, The Grapes of Wrath, which also addresses themes pertinent to the Great Depression

• consider other books that have been censored or banned, such as To Kill a Mockingbird

• compare with other iconic works of American literature from the 1930s, such as Fitzgerald's Tender Is the Night

• compare to Old Yeller, another example of a character being forced to kill something he loves

• compare to Rainman, a film about the love between a mentally handicapped man and the man who helps him through life.

• compare to One Flew Over The Cuckoo's Nest, another example of a mercy kill to prevent a character from suffering a worse life

Teaching Guide - Notes to the Teacher

Teachers should be sure to include information regarding Steinbeck's original intentions for the book (as a stage play, with the original title of *Something That Happened*. By being aware of such information, students can better evaluate the meaning of the text, as well as its final iteration as a novella.

Students will be able to draw upon their experiences of social inequality, whether with peers in school or in larger contexts. In addition, students can consider their own personal friendships and difficult conflicts that may have arisen.

Of Mice and Men can also be used as a means to peripherally study U.S. history and the Great Depression. It can be compared to Steinbeck's *The Grapes of Wrath* to identify similar themes and consider his development as an author. In addition, the work can be used to discuss relevant issues of movie or play adaptations of literature.

Day 1 - Reading Assignment

Students read Part I.

Daily Lesson Objectives

- • Introduction to reading well: learning how to get acquainted with a new work of literature by examining characters, character relationships, tone, and setting; identifying early themes; appreciating the achievement of good writing.

- • Introduction to thinking well: using the discussion questions to do more than just read.

- • Introduction to speaking well: developing oral skills through vocabulary development and discussion of thought questions.

Note that it is perfectly fine to expand any day's work into two days depending on the characteristics of the class, particularly if the class will engage in all of the suggested classroom exercises and activities and discuss all of the thought questions.

Content Summary for Teachers

Part I:

Readers are introduced to the two main characters, George Milton and Lennie Small. The two men have arrived near their next place of work, a ranch. They are close friends, and though Lennie's simple-mindedness frustrates George, the smaller man cares for the enormous Lennie and takes care of him.

It is hinted that the men had to leave their previous employment because Lennie accidentally frightened a young woman by physically clinging to her. Lennie is depicted as being mentally handicapped, at least to some extent. He must follow very simple instructions given by George. At their place of new employment, Lennie is not to speak unless absolutely necessary.

He also has a penchant for touching soft things; George forces him to give up a dead mouse he keeps in his pocket. However, George relents when Lennie asks him to tell him about their dream of owning a ranch, where they will breed rabbits. George describes the ranch in rich detail, with Lennie contributing favorite lines of the recitation - it is a fairy tale they have repeated to each other many times before.

George instructs Lennie that if anything goes awry at this new ranch, Lennie must return to this exact spot where they are camping for the night.

Thought Questions (students consider while they read)

1. Compare and contrast the personalities of George Milton and Lennie Small.
2. Discuss the relationship between George and Lennie; why do you think they are friends?
3. What is the importance of the place by the river?
4. What is the significance of the rabbits?
5. Discuss the dream/story that Lennie asks George to describe for him.

Vocabulary (in order of appearance)

Part I:

- debris: litter, trash; remnants of something that has been destroyed
- mottled: spotted; marked by blotches of color
- recumbent: in the position of lying down
- heron: a type of long-necked and long-legged bird
- bindle: a bundle of clothes and/or bedding materials; during this period in American history, migrant workers like George & Lennie were often called bindlestiffs
- morose: being gloomy or sullen
- pantomime: to convey a story through bodily/facial expressions in a dramatic manner
- imperious: having the air of being arrogantly assured
- anguished: expressing or suffering from agony
- yammer: to make repeated cries, usually of distress

Additional Homework

1. Using a California map, pinpoint the area where Lennie and George are. Compare this location to where Steinbeck was born.
2. The opening of the novella is written in present tense, though the rest of the novel is in past tense. Why do you think Steinbeck did this? One paragraph.

Day 1 - Discussion of Thought Questions

1. Compare and contrast the personalities of George Milton and Lennie Small.

Time: 5 minutes

Discussion:

George Milton should be described as the smaller, more intelligent man. Physically, his features are sharp and well defined, and he is significantly smaller than Lennie. George is more self-aware and goal-oriented, as he plans for their future.

Make note of the irony of Lennie's name. Lennie Small--his name is misleading because he is anything *but* small--is an extraordinarily large man. However, he has the mind of a child and appears to suffer from some form of mental retardation. Lennie is childlike and gentle in nature, but he possesses great physical strength, over which he has little control.

2. Discuss the relationship between George and Lennie; why do you think they are friends?

Time: 10 minutes

Discussion:

Lennie is quite simple-minded, so George often gives him orders and instructions that Lennie *must* obey. At times, George speaks sharply to Lennie, as if he were a child. At the same time, George displays genuine care for Lennie, who trusts his friend wholly. Lennie perceives that he is sometimes a burden to George, and George does not hide his frustrations. Nonetheless, the men share a genuine friendship which began when Lennie's aunt entrusted him to George's care. The two men share a dream: a better life on their own homestead, where Lennie will be permitted to raise rabbits.

Lennie needs George because he is too dim-witted to manage his own affairs and stay out of (inadvertent) trouble. Already in this first section, it is hinted that Lennie was involved in a dangerous issue at their previous place of employment that caused their departure. However, Lennie's presence also makes George feel empowered. Lennie is someone George can instruct and who must obey him. Lennie's clear prowess as a worker also increases the diminutive George's stature and bargaining position at each workplace.

3. What is the importance of the place by the river?

Time: 5-10 minutes

Discussion: *Of Mice and Men* opens with a very vivid and nature-filled description of a hillside bank. Steinbeck's attention to the fresh details of the place--he describes the trees, play of light, and animals in the area--imbue it with a nearly heavenly quality. The fact that George and Lennie choose to stay here for the night, instead of going directly to work as necessary, is significant. This place represents a safe haven to them. This is reinforced by George's instruction to Lennie that if trouble arises, he must return to this place, their retreat from the outer world.

4. What is the significance of the rabbits?

Time: 10 minutes

Discussion: Rabbits first appear as part of the scenery, present at the riverbank when George and Lennie arrive. They are a part of the natural surroundings, emphasizing the sense of nature and safety in this location. Then, when George recounts to Lennie--at the latter's request--their vision of the future, it becomes apparent that rabbits represent to Lennie the hope of a better life. The rabbits represent the men's shared dream to earn enough money to own a ranch and to live and work for themselves. Furthermore, the rabbits possess soft fur, which is significant because Lennie has a strong and dangerous attraction to soft materials. His love of softness represents both his idealized future and his downfall.

5. Discuss the dream/story that Lennie asks George to describe for him.

Time: 5 minutes

Discussion: Lennie begs George to retell the vision of their future, and this is clearly an important ritual, like storytelling to a child. "George's voice became deeper. He repeated his words rhythmically as though he had said them many times before." As George points out, "'You got it by heart. You can do it yourself.'" However, the ritual of storytelling reinforces the bond. These men share the same dream of an idyllic future. This vision drives them to undergo the hardships of migrant workers, but binds them together because the dream is nothing with only one of them.

Day 1 - Short Answer Quiz

1. In what state does *Of Mice and Men* take place?

_____

2. Describe three characteristics of George Milton.

_____

3. Describe three characteristics of Lennie Small.

_____

4. What does Lennie try to hide from George in his pocket?

_____

5. George tells Lennie that if anyone speaks to him at the new ranch, he must:

_____

6. Where must Lennie go if they encounter any trouble at the new ranch?

_____

7. What type of animal does Lennie want to raise in the future, when he owns a home with George?

_____

8. Where are George and Lennie going?

_____

9. What complaint does George have about their bus driver?

_____

10. What does Lennie want with his can of beans?

_____

11. In what location were George and Lennie previously, from which they were forced to leave?

_____

Short Answer Quiz Key

1. California
2. -small

   -sharp features

   -intelligent

   -takes care of Lennie

   -sometimes abrupt toward Lennie
3. -extremely large

   -mentally handicapped

   -very gentle

   -childlike in nature

   -obeys and trusts George
4. a dead mouse
5. remain silent
6. Lennie must return to this location by the river.
7. rabbits
8. To a new ranch, where they will work
9. The driver did not drop them off close enough to the ranch, so they were forced to walk some of the distance.
10. ketchup
11. Weed

Day 1 - Vocabulary Quiz

Terms

1. ____ He saw a ____ wading in the river.
2. ____ The tornado ravaged the house, and its _____ was hardly salvageable.
3. ____ Her face was ____ with acne.
4. ____ Lennie carried his ____ easily because he was such a large man.
5. ____ The woman forbade her son to get the toy, so he became ____.
6. ____ The king waved for his servants with an ____ air.
7. ____ Her voice was ____, as she recounted that her house had been burglarized.
8. ____ The lazy boy was ____ under the tree, his eyes closed as he napped.
9. ____ She enjoyed _____, so charades was the perfect game for the party.
10. ____ Locked outside in the rain, the wet dog began to ____.

Answers

A. recumbent
B. yammer
C. pantomime
D. morose
E. imperious
F. heron
G. mottled
H. bindle
I. debris
J. anguished

Vocabulary Quiz Answer Key

1. F
2. I
3. G
4. H
5. D
6. E
7. J
8. A
9. C
10. B

Day 1 - Classroom Activities

1. Discussion of Conflict

   Kind of Activity: small groups
   Objective: to examine the tensions in the friendship between George and Lennie
   Time: 20 minutes

   Structure:

   Divide the class into groups of four to five students. Instruct them to discuss at least three sources of tension evident in George and Lennie's relationship. These may include: the dead mouse in Lennie's pocket; the ketchup; Lennie's instructions not to speak; how Lennie restricts George's freedom, and vice versa; Lennie's action causing them to leave their previous place of employment, etc.

   Then, the students should discuss how the men overcome these sources of tension to conclude the chapter with the reiterated shared vision of their future together.

   The students should draw upon their own experiences with peers; what are effective ways of handling conflicts with friends? Each group should identify three effective ways of managing conflict to preserve friendship, and compare these suggestions with those employed by George and Lennie.

   The above can be expressed on a shared piece of paper, one page per group, or in brief explanations to the class.

   Assessment Criteria:

   + that the students can pinpoint precise sources of conflict in the characters' friendship

   + that the students perceive how these sources of tension are overcome

   + that the students can relate the theme from the novella to their own lives and personal experiences

2. The Great Depression

   Kind of Activity: classroom discussion

Objective: to understand the setting of *Of Mice and Men* and how it relates to Steinbeck's personal experiences

Time: 10-15 minutes

Structure:

Steinbeck also worked as a migrant worker, or "bindlestiff," during his youth in California. He is thus able to depict with poignant insight the hardships and lonely lives of men like George Milton and Lennie Small. Present the students with information regarding the Great Depression in the United States, and how this might have affected people like George and Lennie. Why might factors in their background force them to become migrant workers?

The United States has recently experienced an economic downturn. Is there any modern equivalent of people like Lennie and George in today's workforce?

What might have motivated Steinbeck to write about the lives of migrant workers during the Great Depression? What message might Steinbeck attempted to impart, in relation to his own experiences?

Assessment Criteria:

+ that students understand the context in which *Of Mice and Men* was written and how this context relates to the author's biography

+ that students observe current events and compare them with this significant period in American history

+ that students fully understand what George and Lennie must do in order to make a living

Day 2 - Reading Assignment

Students read Part II.

Daily Lesson Objectives

• • Work on reading well: learning how to track developing themes and new characters; appreciating the narrative structure of good writing.

• Introduction to thinking well: using the discussion questions to do more than just read; assessing the oral reading of peers.

• Introduction to speaking well: developing oral skills through vocabulary development, discussion of thought questions, and reading aloud.

• Interpretive skills: picking up on subtle clues to determine the tone of the novel and what this section may foreshadow

• Understanding subtle social interactions: considering the role of each new character in relation to the ranch, and in relation to the main characters.

• Introduction to significant themes/symbols: examining social inequalities among the new characters; paying attention to the symbolism of Steinbeck's descriptions of light versus darkness.

Note that it is perfectly fine to expand any day's work into two days depending on the characteristics of the class, particularly if the class will engage in all of the suggested classroom exercises and activities and discuss all of the thought questions.

Content Summary for Teachers

Part II:

Like the previous section, this part opens with a richly detailed description of the new setting: the bunkhouse, where George and Lennie will live while they work at this ranch. The scene is very sunny, as Candy enters the bunkhouse followed by the newly arrived protagonists. Candy informs them that the ranch boss was angry they did not arrive yesterday, as expected. He tells them the boss can be difficult and often abuses the stable boy, an older black man.

The boss arrives and asks questions of George and Lennie. Only George responds, and the boss grows suspicious of their relationship. He wonders if George is taking advantage of Lennie, i.e., perhaps stealing his money. George fibs that Lennie is his cousin and was kicked in the head as a child. The boss leaves, and George rebukes Lennie for speaking to the boss at all. Candy overhears them, but he does not seem to want to cause trouble.

The boss's son Curley arrives. He is antagonistic and arrogant; he also questions the relationship between the protagonists, as well as Lennie's reticence. After he leaves, Candy explains to George and Lennie that Curley has recently been married, but his wife consistently flirts with the other ranch workers. George seriously warns Lennie to stay away from Curley at all costs.

Curley's wife arrives, blocking the light that streams into the bunkhouse through the doorway. She is definitely interested in the new arrivals. Lennie is fascinated by her, but not necessarily in a sexual manner. Again, George warns Lennie to stay away from Curley's wife.

Then, other ranch workers arrive: Slim and Carlson. Slim is described as a respectable, quiet and strong individual; he carries a much more positive aura than Curley and previous characters. Slim's dog has just had puppies, and Lennie hopes to have one.

Thought Questions (students consider while they read)

1. The previous section took place at one location: the riverside bank. This scene is contained in the bunkhouse. Discuss the significance of this, given the novella's original form.
2. Why are so many people apparently suspicious of George and Lennie's friendship?
3. What distinguishes Slim from the other men?
4. What is significant about the appearance of Curley's wife and Lennie's reaction to her?
5. In the middle of this section, Steinbeck writes:

   "Lennie cried out suddenly--'I don' like this place, George. This ain't no good place. I wanna get outta here.'"

   Discuss the significance of this quote, given the new characters that are introduced in this section.

Vocabulary (in order of appearance)

Part II:

- burlap: a plain, thick and heavy fabric; in this context, used for bedding
- vial: a small, circular container used to store liquids
- pants rabbits and greybacks: lice and cockroaches
- skeptical: disbelieving

- liniment: a liquid solution applied to the skin as medical ointment
- relish: satisfaction
- rassle: wrestle
- grizzled: streaked with gray
- pugnacious: quarrelsome, belligerent
- derogatory: demeaning in nature; expressing a poor opinion of something
- Solitaire: a card game designed for one person to play alone
- arch (adjective): forced playfulness; flirtatious
- apprehensive: nervous or alarmed by the future
- complacent: satisfied to the point of unconcern

Additional Homework

1. Have the students do basic Internet research about migrant workers in the United States during the Great Depression. Pick one of the characters (i.e., Slim or Lennie) and identify their role on the ranch. Then learn more about what that role entails in terms of responsibilities. The students should write one paragraph about the information they have gathered.

Day 2 - Discussion of Thought Questions

1. The previous section took place at one location: the riverside bank. This scene is contained in the bunkhouse. Discuss the significance of this, given the novella's original form.

   Time: 5 minutes

   Discussion: Remind students that Steinbeck originally intended *Of Mice and Men* as a stage play. Thus, students should begin to think of the novella in play form. This is reflected in the simple and stationary sets. Characters move in and out of the scene, but the setting remains stagnant, which makes the direction of a stage play more feasible.

2. Why are so many people apparently suspicious of George and Lennie's friendship?

   Time: 10 minutes

   Discussion: First, the discussion should identify which characters find their relationship suspicious: Candy, the unnamed ranch boss, and Curley. Discuss potential reasons for such suspicion and what speculations these men might bear. Migrant workers are depicted as tough, solitary, and lonesome. The fact that two unrelated men might choose to remain together and to maintain a friendship is difficult for such workers to comprehend. As a result, the ranch boss wonders whether George is exploiting Lennie's labor and stealing his pay, or otherwise benefiting unethically from their relationsihp.

3. What distinguishes Slim from the other men?

   Time: 5 minutes

   Discussion: Descriptions of Slim are full of words like "majesty, "master," "dignity," etc. More specifically, Steinbeck writes, "His authority was so great that his word was taken on any subject." Unlike the ranch boss and Curley, who must wear high-heeled boots to distinguish themselves as bearing power, Slim's authority is intangible but unquestionable. This is reinforced at the end of the section when Carlson follows Slim outside. Furthermore, Slim appears to be a clean and respectable character; he does not foreshadow danger, as do Curley and his wife.

4. What is significant about the appearance of Curley's wife and Lennie's reaction to her?

Time: 10 minutes

Discussion:

Candy has already provided information to indicate that Curley's wife is a flirt, and that most of the men choose to ignore her. Curley seems to be aware of his wife's tendency to be unfaithful in spirit, if not in action. As an extremely belligerent and unreasonable man, this foreshadows danger.

Likewise, when Curley's wife first appears (she also remains nameless throughout the novella), she blocks off the light streaming into the bunkhouse. Before this, George, Lennie and Candy are getting along quite amicably. Her arrival, blocking the natural sunlight, hints at the danger she represents. Sunlight is used in the novella to indicate freshness, nature, peace and safety; it suffuses the riverbank in the first section, and opens this chapter in the bunkhouse.

Lennie's fascination with Curley's wife does not bode well. The men encountered trouble in Weed because of a woman. Again, this is another example of Steinbeck's use of foreshadowing.

5. In the middle of this section, Steinbeck writes:

"Lennie cried out suddenly--'I don' like this place, George. This ain't no good place. I wanna get outta here.'"

Discuss the significance of this quote, given the new characters that are introduced in this section.

Time: 10 minutes

Discussion:

Despite Lennie's simplicity of mind, he senses the undercurrent of danger that runs at this bunkhouse. He keenly recognizes, whether or not intentionally, the dangers represented by Curley and his wife. Although there are benign characters, such as Candy and Slim, they are offset by the foreshadowing of future events that may derail George and Lennie's plans.

Furthermore, the bunkhouse is wholly unlike their natural haven, described in the first section. The bunkhouse is a manmade, enclosed space. The door must be open to allow in sunlight. Lennie recognizes the "trappings" of this place, subject to the customs of society, and wishes to be free, where he can pet mice and dream about growing rabbits.

Day 2 - Short Answer Quiz

1. Name at least three new characters who are introduced in this chapter.

_____

2. What time of day is it when this section starts?

_____

3. Why is George suspicious of his sleeping area?

_____

4. List two qualities about the stable boy.

_____

5. George lies to the ranch boss and says that Lennie and he are related in what way?

_____

6. The swamper owns what kind of pet?

_____

7. Curley wears only one of what accessory?

_____

8. What card game does George play in this section?

_____

9. What event does Carlson ask Slim about near the end of the section?

_____

10. Who is Lennie instructed to avoid?

_____

Short Answer Quiz Key

1. Candy

   Curley

   Curley's wife

   Slim

   Carlson

   the ranch boss
2. Mid-morning.
3. It may contain bedbugs, lice and cockroaches.
4. He is African American. He has a crooked back.
5. cousins
6. Dog
7. glove
8. Solitaire
9. Slim's dog having puppies
10. Curley and Curley's wife

Day 2 - Vocabulary Quiz

Terms	Answers

Terms

1. ____ She held up a small ____ of green liquid.
2. ____ The ___ sack was sturdy and able to hold many groceries.
3. ____ The doctor applied ___ to soothe the burn on his hand.
4. ____ Already in a bad mood, the clerk became ___ as he dealt with the complaining customer.
5. ____ Her ___ remarks were quite offensive.
6. ____ Her sister was at school, so she took out her cards to play ____.
7. ____ As finals' week approached, the procrastinator became _____.
8. ____ disbelieving
9. ____ bedbugs/lice and cockroaches
10. ____ satisfaction
11. ____ marked with gray streakss
12. ____ to wrestle
13. ____ forcefully playful
14. ____ self-satisfied

Answers

A. pugnacious
B. derogatory
C. Solitaire
D. burlap
E. relish
F. rassle
G. skeptical
H. apprehensive
I. liniment
J. arch
K. grizzled
L. pants rabbits and greybacks
M. vial
N. complacent

Vocabulary Quiz Answer Key

1. M
2. D
3. I
4. A
5. B
6. C
7. H
8. G
9. L
10. E
11. K
12. F
13. J
14. N

Day 2 - Classroom Activities

1. Drawing the Bunkhouse

Kind of Activity: individual
Objective: to pay attention to descriptive details and exercise artistic skills
Time: 20 minutes

Structure:

Of Mice and Men is structured like a stage play, with each section taking place in a single location. Carefully review the details of the bunkhouse - both the description of its appearance and the way it is used in the action. Have students discuss what features of the room need to be in the forefront and where most of the action would play. Whose bunks do we need to see clearly? Which doors and windows are important?

After the discussion, instruct students to draw their set design for the bunkhouse. For extra credit, offer the option of building a diorama or model.

Assessment Criteria:

+ that students have noticed details in the text regarding the description of the bunkhouse

+ that students employ creativity, imagination and artistic skills to render this understanding of the text into a picture

2. Discussion of Social Inequalities

Kind of Activity: class discussion
Objective: to highlight the theme of social inequality, using examples from the text
Time: 15-20 minutes

Structure: Examine the descriptions of the stable boy and of Curley's wife, both by the narrative voice and by individual characters. How are these characters described? Positively or negatively, and why? What does this have to do with the fact that Curley's wife is a woman, and that the stable boy is not white?

Assessment Criteria:

+ that students can draw examples from the text to support their opinions

+ that students understand the meaning of inequality

+ that students perceive the significance of such social inequality during this period in American history

+ that students are able to make reasonable inferences from the text

Day 3 - Reading Assignment

Students read Part III.

Daily Lesson Objectives

- 1. Reading well: continuing to track themes; examining character development (especially as George and Lennie are seen interacting with other characters and a dramatic event occurs); appreciating how the novella continues to resemble stageplay format.

  2. Thinking well: re-envisioning this chapter as it would be presented in a play or film and condensing the dialogue/action to do so; thus, students must be able to discern only the most pertinent details of the chapter to construct a concise and meaningful mini-script.

  3. Speaking well: developing oral skills through vocabulary development, dramatic readings, and group discussion.

  4. Listening well: assessing the dramatic readings; developing a taste for good grammar and strong diction; evaluating the arguments of other groups in the discussion activity.

  5. Understanding: identifying how dramatically the plot has progressed with definite action since the first two scenes; exploring the existing themes regarding inequality, futile dreams, and fate.

Note that it is perfectly fine to expand any day's work into two days depending on the characteristics of the class, particularly if the class will engage in all of the suggested classroom exercises and activities and discuss all of the thought questions.

Content Summary for Teachers

Part III:

The chapter opens with a very frank talk between George and Slim, in which the latter talks about his history with Lennie and how they came to be friends. George also explains the exact event that caused them to leave their previous job. Lennie held on to a girl's dress because it was soft. When she panicked, he too grew alarmed and held the dress more tightly. He was accused of rape, so George and Lennie escaped the false charges.

Then, the other ranch workers return to the bunkhouse, where they play a game called horseshoes. Carlson complains about the stink of Candy's dog, which is extremely old and sick, and suggests that they shoot the dog. Candy is reluctant because he has owned the dog since it was born and is very attached to the pet. However, Carlson insists and offers to shoot the dog himself. Finally, Candy complies and Carlson takes the dog outside with a gun. The atmosphere in the bunkhouse is extremely tense as the men await the sound of the gunshot.

Crooks appears, and he warns Lennie (who has been given possession of one of the puppies from Slim's new litter) not to touch the puppies. They are too young to be handled roughly. Then, another man named Whit turns the discussion to Curley's wife. Whit invites George to visit a brothel with the men in town, the next time they go. Carlson has returned to the bunkhouse.

Curley is looking for his wife and suspects that she is in the barn with Slim. Anticipating a showdown, most of the workers follow Curley there. At the bunkhouse, Lennie asks George to recount the description of their dream home and the rabbits. Candy, still struck by the abrupt loss of his dog, listens to them. He joins their plan; with his money, their dream is attainable, and sooner than expected. Candy mentions that he wishes he shot his dog himself.

The men return to the bunkhouse, with Curley apologizing to Slim. Carlson and Candy mock Curley's cowardice. Meanwhile, Lennie is still smiling over the memory of the discussion about the ranch. Curley leaps upon this as an opportunity to attack Lennie. George commands Lennie to defend himself, and frightened, Lennie grabs Curley's fist. In his fright and uncontrollable strength, Lennie crushes Curley's fist. Curley is dispatched to the doctor by Slim and Carlson. Slim makes Curley promise not to tell anyone what actually happened, or the other men will make Curley a laughingstock.

Thought Questions (students consider while they read)

1. George explains to Slim more about his relationship with Lennie. How would you characterize it? How has it changed since they first met, according to George?
2. What do you think about the death of Candy's dog? Why might it be significant to the story?
3. Why does Curley decide to pick on Lennie at the end of the chapter?
4. Why do you think Slim intervenes in the situation regarding Curley's injured hand to protect Lennie? Who is this incident, in which Lennie crushes Curley's hand, foreshadowed earlier in the section?
5. Given the way the men discuss women--Curley's wife and the brothel--what can you glean about their personal lives?
6. Explore Candy's reasons for wanting to join George and Lennie, when they finally have enough money to buy their own place.

Vocabulary (in order of appearance)

Part III:

- barley: a cereal grass
- nuisance: a bother; an annoyance
- scuttle: to scurry
- pulp magazine: cheap magazines featuring fictional stories or comics
- euchre: a type of card game involving multiple players
- Kewpie doll: doll based on illustrations by Rose O'Neill that first appeared in 1909, which is characterized by puckered lips and a heart-shaped face
- San Quentin: a jail in California
- jail bait: an underage woman, usually, or any woman who is likely to drive a man to illegal or dangerous action
- reverent: expressing awe, admiration
- bemused: tolerantly amused
- slug: to punch

Additional Homework

1. Examine the area where this novella takes place on a map. What nearby towns are there (that existed in the 1930s), to which the men could be referring? Identify one such town and do some background research on its history, particularly during the 1930s. Write two paragraphs, the first of which describes why this town could plausibly be the one described in *Of Mice and Men*. In the second paragraph, write a brief synopsis of the town's history.
2. This section--which spans the course of one night--is quite eventful for a number of characters. Adopting the perspective of either Candy, George, Curley, or Lennie, write a one-page journal entry about the night's events.

Day 3 - Discussion of Thought Questions

1. George explains to Slim more about his relationship with Lennie. How would you characterize it? How has it changed since they first met, according to George?

   Time: 10 minutes

   Discussion: In the beginning, George admits that he also mocked and took advantage of Lennie because of his mental handicap. However, this changed when George realized how innocently Lennie trusted him. Even when George ordered Lennie to do something as preposterous as jump in a lake, Lennie did so, almost resulting in a fatal accident. After this event, George learned to respect and genuinely care for Lennie instead of abusing him. Now, George feels protective of Lennie against other men who discount him as a fool or as "cuckoo."

2. What do you think about the death of Candy's dog? Why might it be significant to the story?

   Time: 10 minutes

   Discussion:

   The plotted death of Candy's dog, which is extremely old and ill, directly contrasts how Lennie may inadvertently hurt smaller animals. The incident is framed by two mentions of Lennie and the new puppy. First, Lennie returns to the bunkhouse with a puppy hidden in his coat; George orders him to return the puppy to its mother so that it can be properly raised. He warns Lennie that he will hurt the puppy.

   Then, Carlson persuades Candy to let him shoot his dog. This is a premeditated death.

   Thereafter, Crooks appears in the bunkhouse. Like George, he also warns Lennie not to touch the pups because he may hurt them. The two differing events, involving the deaths of dogs, highlight Lennie's capacity to hurt smaller creatures in his misplaced enthusiasm and uncontrolled/unknown strength.

3. Why does Curley decide to pick on Lennie at the end of the chapter?

Time: 5 minutes

Discussion: Curley is humiliated in front of the other men. Carlson and Candy are already mocking him for being a coward. He must apologize to Slim, while also admitting that he *does* suspect that something illicit may be going on between Slim and his own wife. Thus, Curley is in a defensive position and wishes to strike out. This is in line with his personality described in the previous section by Candy. Lennie is an easy target.

4. Why do you think Slim intervenes in the situation regarding Curley's injured hand to protect Lennie? Who is this incident, in which Lennie crushes Curley's hand, foreshadowed earlier in the section?

Time: 5 minutes

Discussion: After talking to George, and being a man of good judgment himself, Slim recognizes Lennie for what he is: a gentle, good-hearted, child-like man who is not aware of his own strength. Everyone knows that Lennie (and possibly George) would be fired if the incident is made known to the ranch boss. Thus, Slim wishes to protect this innocent man; the incident is reminiscent of what Slim has just learned about the girl in Weed who falsely accused Lennie of rape.

5. Given the way the men discuss women--Curley's wife and the brothel--what can you glean about their personal lives?

Time: 10 minutes

Discussion: The nature of their work makes it seemingly inevitable that these migrant workers are lonely and isolated from one another. Their relationships with other people, men and women, are at most superficial friendships, born of location and convenience. That is why so many are confounded by George's closeness with Lennie. Likewise, they do not view women as potential lifelong companions. These men seem to have resigned themselves to their solitude. Women are only viewed as potential passing diversions.

6. Explore Candy's reasons for wanting to join George and Lennie, when they finally have enough money to buy their own place.

Time: 10-15 minutes

Discussion: Candy's character exemplifies running themes in the novella: loneliness and inequality. Due to his physical limitations and his age, Candy is not respected on the ranch. Carlson's killing of Candy's dog is another example of how the men do not respect him. He suffers from social inequality, and as a character separate from the younger, healthier and abler ranch workers, Candy is isolated. He too suffers from loneliness and jumps at the chance to join George and Lennie. He is even willing to leave his will to them, in order to gain their trust, and to contribute money toward purchasing the homestead.

Day 3 - Short Answer Quiz

1. Who is the only new character introduced in this section?

_____

2. What do the men do as they pass the time waiting for the gunshot signifying that Candy's dog has been killed?

_____

3. Why did George initially begin spending time with Lennie?

_____

4. What event changed George's first attitude toward Lennie?

_____

5. What was the color of the girl's dress in Weed, who later accused Lennie of rape?

_____

6. What seems to happen when Lennie is holding something but becomes frightened?

_____

7. Name two reasons Carlson cites to convince Candy that his dog should be killed.

_____

8. How does Carlson kill Candy's dog?

_____

9. Where are the puppies kept?

_____

10. George and Lennie have their eye on an existing ranch to buy. How much would it cost?

_____

11. As the other men return to the bunkhouse, what does George warn Lennie and Candy, regarding their dream ranch?

_____

12. What does Curley do to Lennie before Lennie crushes his hand?

_____

Short Answer Quiz Key

1. Whit
2. Play euchre, a card game
3. In the beginning, Lennie's simple-mindedness made George feel good about himself.
4. Lennie almost drowned, simply because he jumped into a lake at George's bidding.
5. red
6. He clings to it/crushes it.
7. The dog smells bad. The dog suffers from rheumatism. The dog is suffering and should be put out of his misery.
8. He shoots it.
9. in the barn
10. $600
11. not to tell anyone else about their plan to compile their savings.
12. Curley punches Lennie repeatedly in the face and torso.

Day 3 - Vocabulary Quiz

Terms

1. ____ type of grass
2. ____ to hit, to punch
3. ____ a type of card game
4. ____ a jail in California
5. ____ a bother, an annoyance
6. ____ expressing awe or admiration
7. ____ a cheap magazine that features short fiction or comics
8. ____ to scurry
9. ____ a brand-name doll modeled after a 1909 comic

Answers

A. scuttle
B. euchre
C. barley
D. San Quentin Jail
E. pulp magazine
F. nuisance
G. reverent
H. Kewpie doll
I. slug

Vocabulary Quiz Answer Key

1. C
2. I
3. B
4. D
5. F
6. G
7. E
8. A
9. H

Day 3 - Classroom Activities

1. Dramatizing the Text

   Kind of Activity: small groups
   Objective: to envision the text, as Steinbeck originally did, as a stageplay instead of a narrative novella
   Time: 40 minutes

   Structure:

   This section can be divided into several dialogue chunks, as follows:

   1. George, Slim, Lennie and Candy (discussing Lennie)

   2. Candy and Carlson (discussing the dog)

   3. George, Lennie and Candy (discussing the dream)

   4. Curley, George, Lennie and Slim (the fight)

   Divide the class into four groups, and assign a scene to each group.

   Together, the students should develop a script for each scene, based on the dialogue in Steinbeck's text. The scripts will be of variable length, depending on the students' decisions about what lines are necessary to dramatize the scene. Reinforce the importance of stage directions - in a dramatic script, visuals are just as important as words, and a lot can be said with a few well-chosen gestures.

   Assessment Criteria:

   + understanding of the key points of dialogue and action

   + ability to paraphrase such points into a viable working script

   + understanding of the play/screenplay format

2. Acting Out the Text

   Kind of Activity: small groups, class presentation
   Objective: to act out the scripts created in the previous activity
   Time: 30 minutes

Structure:

Reassign the class into four different groups, with combinations of students that are different from those in the previous assignment.

Allow the students to take 10 minutes to prepare their dramatization of each script, with students assigned to act out each part. Students can double up on parts if there are not enough characters to go around.

Each scene should then be acted out in chronological order before the class.

Afterwards, the students should discuss which scenes were adapted and dramatized most successfully which scenes could be improved and why, etc. Focus on Steinbeck's original intent to make this a stage play, as well as the real adaptations into a play and film. How does the text lend itself to such adaptations?

Assessment Criteria:

+ understanding the nature of adaptations from texts

+ assessing other students' scripts and dramatizations

+ listening intently to discussion and constructive criticism

+ full understanding of the pertinent aspects of the text in this section

+ perceiving tension in character dialogue

Day 4 - Reading Assignment

Students read Part IV.

Daily Lesson Objectives

- • Reading well: appreciating the next "scene" or "stage setting" in the drama, which features less action but positions the characters for the upcoming climax.

- Thinking well: using the discussion questions and analysis of character interactions to identify the themes of loneliness and inequality in seemingly dissimilar characters.

- Speaking well: developing oral skills through vocabulary development, debate, and group discussion.

- Listening well: developing a taste for good grammar and strong diction by closely examining other students' representations of these characters and evaluating oral arguments in the classroom activities.

- Writing well: creating and sustaining an argument, using evidence, in essay form.

- Understanding: seeing how themes of social inequality (particularly race and gender), loneliness, and unfulfilled dreams, friendship, place, and fate are highlighted in this relatively expository chapter that features little drama.

Note that it is perfectly fine to expand any day's work into two days depending on the characteristics of the class, particularly if the class will engage in all of the suggested classroom exercises and activities and discuss all of the thought questions.

Content Summary for Teachers

Part IV:

As usual, this section opens with a thorough description of the setting: Crooks's living space, which is a small shed attached to the barn. Crooks is tending to his back on a Saturday night, when Lennie appears. The other men have gone into town to party, and Lennie is lonely. Initially, Crooks is unwelcoming, but eventually, her permits Lennie to enter and sit.

Lennie tells Crooks about the rabbits and the dream about the future home, but Crooks does not understand him and scoffs at the notion. In the meantime, Crooks tells Lennie about his childhood, the discrimination he has faced, and his general loneliness. Ironically, the men are confiding very personal information to one another, but neither truly pays attention to the other.

Jealous of Lennie and George's friendship, Crooks goads Lennie into wondering what would happen if George did not return from town--either out of malice or out of injury. Lennie becomes very upset. Then, Candy arrives, as he too has been excluded from the other men's activities. Together, Candy and Lennie tell Crooks about their plan to purchase a farm together. Crooks, initially disbelieving, wants to join them when he learns this is a viable plan.

Suddenly, Curley's wife appears under the guise of looking for Curley. Candy and Crooks, sensing the trouble she inevitably brings, are unwelcoming. Lennie is simply fascinated by her beauty. Curley's wife breaks into an outburst about her own loneliness and isolation in an unhappy marriage.

Crooks orders her to leave, and she reminds him that she can have him hanged if she were to accuse him of anything. All three men subside, their earlier joy about the dream dissipated. Curley's wife reveals that she knows Lennie is the reason behind Curley's injured hand.

The other men return from town. Curley's wife leaves. George is angry to discover that Candy and Lennie have revealed their plan to Crooks. However, Crooks withdraws his desire to join them. Cyclically, the chapter ends as it begins--with Crooks alone in his room, tending to his back.

Thought Questions (students consider while they read)

1. Why do you think Crooks is unwelcoming to Lennie when he first appears?
2. What do you notice about the conversation between Crooks and Lennie?
3. Why does Crooks try to make Lennie doubt whether George will come back? What is interesting about Lennie's reaction?
4. What are the similarities and differences between the four characters featured in this section?
5. Why is it important to George that the plan be kept a secret between Candy, George and Lennie?

Vocabulary (in order of appearance)

Part IV:

- stable buck: a stable boy; one who works in the stable to tend to the horses, etc.
- hame: curved support attached to the collar on a horse

- accumulate: to gather in increments
- aloof: distant
- alfalfa: a type of plant
- contemptuous: expressing disgust and/or lack of respect
- indignation: anger or the feeling of being upset due to an injustice or some perceived wrongdoing
- baloney: nonsense
- appraise: to assess
- crestfallen: feeling shame or disappointment

Additional Homework

1. Research information regarding the treatment of either women or of African Americans (select one) during the Great Depression in California. In what ways did this group of people face discrimination? How did this group attempt to combat such discrimination? Has such discrimination fully dissipated in current society, or not? Write a three paragraph essay to address each topic.

Day 4 - Discussion of Thought Questions

1. Why do you think Crooks is unwelcoming to Lennie when he first appears?

Time: 10 minutes

Discussion: Crooks, as he describes later in the chapter, has been accustomed to racial discrimination and segregation. The men do not ordinarily include him in their activities. He is looked down upon simply because he is African American. Years of these experiences have hardened Crooks against offers of friendship. He is suspicious of Lennie because he has learned to close himself off from any companionship. Crooks masks his true loneliness by adopting the attitude that he does not need other people, hence his initial reception to Lennie.

2. What do you notice about the conversation between Crooks and Lennie?

Time: 10 minutes

Discussion:

Eager for human interaction, Crooks reveals much to Lennie about his youth, growing up as an African American, and his adulthood, during which he has also faced racial discrimination and felt quite lonely. Likewise, Lennie reveals a lot of information about his plan with George to own a home and raise rabbits, etc.

However, the men do not truly *listen* to each other as they speak. Their dialogue runs parallel, and they fail to interact with one another in a meaningful sense. They only begin to engage when Crooks attempts to make Lennie fearful of the strength of his relationship with George.

3. Why does Crooks try to make Lennie doubt whether George will come back? What is interesting about Lennie's reaction?

Time: 5 minutes

Discussion: Crooks is most likely envious of Lennie's apparent closeness with George, as he craves similar human interaction. Thus, he tries to provoke Lennie by causing him to doubt whether George will in fact abandon him or return from town. This is one of the very few times in the novella that Lennie displays any inclination toward violence. Thus, Lennie is equally protective of George; the friendship is mutually supportive, not George always caring for Lennie without reciprocation. Furthermore, Lennie is usually violent by accident; again, this is one of the rare times that he demonstrates the will for violence.

4. What are the similarities and differences between the four characters featured in this section?

Time: 10-15 minutes

Discussion:

All of these characters are victims of social inequality, experience loneliness, and have unfulfilled dreams. The reasons for their experiences, however, are quite different.

As discussed previously, Crooks is the victim of racial discrimination, exacerbated by his physical deformity. He has had a lonely life, although he lives among a community of male ranch workers. They consistently exclude him from their interactions--even his living space is segregated. He dismisses other men's dreams as foolishness, but clearly, Crooks also dreams of a better life for himself. This explains why he jumps at the opportunity to join George, Lennie and Candy.

Candy is treated unequally and likewise excluded from the other men's activities because he is much older and handicapped. He too feels lonely and disrespected. His only faithful companion, the dog, has already been shot and killed by Carlson. Thus, Candy dreams of a life in which he will not be subjected to others' discrimination and lack of respect; however, this dream remains unrealized.

Lennie faces discrimination and inequality because of his lesser mental capabilities, which are obvious. He does have George's friendship, which is a source of comfort, but Lennie remains lonely when George leaves him to spend time with the other men. His dream is to live simply, to live naturally where he will not be constrained by society's customs and expectations. He envisions this at the farm where he will be allowed to raise rabbits.

Finally, Curley's wife is another unexpectedly lonely character, despite being married and lusted after by some of the men. She once dreamed of using her beauty to become a movie star. However, her dreams were unfulfilled because she ended up marrying Curley instead. Now, she is left alone, the sole woman on the ranch, ignored or ostracized by the men, and certainly ignored by her husband. She faces gender discrimination, as the men are aware they cannot associate with her without incurring Curley's wrath.

5. Why is it important to George that the plan be kept a secret between Candy, George and Lennie?

Time: 5-10 minutes

Discussion: George aptly realizes how other men might react to the notion that they could achieve their dream. To these migrant workers, that is a preposterous idea and would like draw a reaction like Crooks's: disbelief and skepticism, if not outright contempt. In order to preserve the sacredness of their dream, they must keep it free from the "taint" of real life. Furthermore, the plan involves money, which could draw unwanted dangerous attention from others. Finally, if the others know of the plan and their intentions to quit the ranch as soon as they receive their pay, they might attempt (out of jealousy/envy) to thwart the plan by getting them fired.

Day 4 - Discussion of Thought Questions

Day 4 - Short Answer Quiz

1. What is Crooks doing when Lennie enters?

_____

2. What day is it in this section?

_____

3. Why isn't Lennie with George?

_____

4. Where was Crooks born, and what did his father own?

_____

5. What is one aspect of loneliness that disturbs Crooks?

_____

6. What transgression do Candy and Lennie share?

_____

7. How does Curley's wife describe the three men, when she first enters the room?

_____

8. Why do you think Curley's wife questions the appearance of bruises on Lenny's face?

_____

9. How does Curley's wife threaten Crooks?

_____

10. Name at least three things the men hope to cultivate at their dream farm.

_____

Short Answer Quiz Key

1. tending to his back pain with liniment
2. Saturday
3. George has joined the other men in town, leaving behind Lennie.
4. California; a chicken ranch
5. He has no other person who can verify his experiences, or with whom he can discuss his thoughts, opinions, etc.
6. They forget George's order not to tell anyone else about their dream, and they tell Crooks.
7. She calls them the "weak ones."
8. She realizes he is the cause behind Curley's injury.
9. She threatens to have him hanged.
10. chickens

   rabbins

   fruit trees

   green corn

   cow

   goat

Day 4 - Vocabulary Quiz

Terms	Answers
1. ____ to assess	A. aloof
2. ____ having an attitude of disgust	B. appraise
	C. crestfallen
3. ____ a type of plant	D. indignation
4. ____ to collect gradually	E. contemptuous
	F. alfalfa
5. ____ a piece of gear used on a horse	G. hame
	H. stable buck
6. ____ disappointed or shamed	I. baloney
	J. accumulate
7. ____ having the air of being distant	
8. ____ nonsense	
9. ____ one who works in a stable	
10. ____ anger generated by some perceived injustice	

Vocabulary Quiz Answer Key

1. B
2. E
3. F
4. J
5. G
6. C
7. A
8. I
9. H
10. D

Day 4 - Classroom Activities

1. In-class Essay Writing

Kind of Activity: individual
Objective: to create a thesis and develop a thorough argument, using evidence from the text, to support the thesis
Time: 30 minutes

Structure:

The students should select one of the characters featured in this section: Crooks, Candy, Lennie or Curley's wife. Which of these characters has most cause to be unhappy, and why? Which of these reasons are external (out of the control of the character) and which are internal (due to the character's personal attributes or attitude toward life)? What could this character plausibly do in order to change his or her situation?

The essay should be five paragraphs in length: introduction, three body paragraphs (for each specific question) and a conclusion.

Assessment Criteria:

+ that students present a clear thesis in the introduction

+ that students use relevant evidence from the text to support the thesis

+ that students develop a clear and logical argument throughout the essay

+ that students are creative but make plausible suggestions for the last question

+ that students use the appropriate vocabulary to express themselves, and that the essays are grammatically correct, well-structured, etc.

2. Reading Aloud: Comparing the Script with the Text

Kind of Activity: small groups
Objective: to practice reading aloud and to hone listening skills in order to evaluate other students' performances
Time: 40 minutes

Structure:

Divide the class into four groups.

Two groups will take the passage starting from: "She looked from one face to another..." and ending at "She slipped out the door and disappeared into the dark barn."

The other two groups will take the passage starting from: "Crooks said irritably, 'You can come in if you want'" to "'You gotta husban'. You got no call foolin' aroun' with other guys, causin' trouble.'"

For each passage, one group will read aloud the text without dramatization. Parts can be assigned for each character and the narrator, depending on the number of students in the class. Make sure every student gets a chance to read aloud.

The other group (for each passage) will dramatize the text. The narration will not be read, only the dialogue, with students positioned/standing to act out the text, as in a dramatic play.

Have the students divide the parts and prepare for 20 minutes. The next 20 should be spent for each group, five minutes per group, to present their reading.

Afterward, lead a discussion regarding which representations are more effective, aurally and visually. Does the expository narration help listeners/viewers to understand? Or is the non-narrated dramatization more effective? Why?

Assessment Criteria:

+ that students develop clear public speaking skills and have good diction

+ that students are listening well to their peers' presentations

+ that students are able to evaluate effective speech-making and acting

+ that students gain better insight to the appropriate intonations and subtleties in the dialogue

Day 5 - Reading Assignment

Students read the rest of the novella (Parts V & VI).

Daily Lesson Objectives

• • Reading well: appreciating the achievement of the author by examining how each theme culminates and interlocks with other themes, and how the author combines tone, dialogue, suspense, and dramatic action to carry the reader's interest.

• Thinking well: using the discussion questions to interpret the text and evaluate the characters' actions, and to consider whether George's actions are justified; assessing the likelihood of alternative depictions of an event.

• Speaking well: developing oral skills through vocabulary development, debate, individual presentation, and group discussion.

• Listening well: developing a taste for good grammar and strong diction; evaluating oral arguments and presentations.

• Writing well: creating and sustaining a descriptive essay, using evidence, in essay form.

• Understanding: seeing how the themes regarding loneliness, unfulfilled dreams, social inequality, and fate have culminated in the dramatic events that conclude this novella.

Note that it is perfectly fine to expand any day's work into two days depending on the characteristics of the class, particularly if the class will engage in all of the suggested classroom exercises and activities and discuss all of the thought questions.

Content Summary for Teachers

Part V:

Most of the men are outside relaxing, but Lennie is in the barn alone. He has accidentally killed his puppy, and he is anxious that this will prevent him from being allowed to raise rabbits.

Curley's wife enters the barn and wants to talk to Lennie. Remembering George's advice, Lennie is initially reluctant. Lennie starts to talk about the dream ranch; the issue of touching soft materials is raised. Curley's wife allows Lennie to teach her hair.

Lennie is not gentle, as expected, and Curley's wife panics that he will mess up her hair. This makes Lennie panic as well, and he holds on to her hair tightly. She screams, and in trying to make Curley's wife be quiet, Lennie accidentally breaks her neck. Lennie perceives that he will be in trouble. He must retreat to the clearing, as George instructed at the beginning of the novella. He takes the dead puppy with him.

Candy discovers the body and calls for George. George realizes that the other men will find out; Lennie will be prosecuted or he will starve to death alone. Candy points out that Curley will want to kill Lennie. The two men recognize that their dream is now impossible. George asks Lennie not to tell the other men that he knows about the accident, so that the men do not think George has conspired with Lennie.

The men discover the death of Curley's wife. Curley wants to hunt down Lennie and shoot him; Carlson agrees. Slim and George consider the possibility of arresting Lennie beforehand so that Curley cannot kill him, but Slim thinks that would be a cruel option as well.

Carlson's gun is missing, and he thinks Lennie has stolen it. However, this is not the case (because George retreated suspiciously to the bunkhouse and emerged, pretending not to know about the death). Everyone assumes Lennie has stolen the gun and is armed; no one is suspicious of George. Now, Lennie must be killed because he is armed.

George tries to convince the men to be lenient if they find Lennie. Curley remains adamant about killing Lennie; he makes George join their manhunt to prove there was no conspiracy.

Part VI:

Lennie sits by the river - the scene opens very much like the beginning of the novella. He hallucinates about his Aunt Clara, who scolds him for being a burden upon George. Lennie also imagines a voice reminding him that there will be no rabbits and that George will leave him.

George arrives, and Lennie expects a punishment. Lennie asks George to say that he would rather be alone. However, George insists that he wishes to be with Lennie, and he recounts the vision of the dream home with rabbits.

George tells Lennie to remove his hat. The two continue talking as George sits behind Lennie. The sound of the other men can be heard as they approach to the riverbank. Finally, George shoots Lennie in the back of the head, just as he receives reassurance about the security of their dream.

The men arrive, and Carlson assumes that George was able to get the gun away from Lennie and shoot him.

As the story closes, Slim and George walk away together - Slim is the only person who can understand George's grief. Curley and Carlson display no compassion.

Thought Questions (students consider while they read)

1. In the opening of Part V, Lennie speaks aloud to the dead puppy in the barn. What does this demonstrate about Lennie and his inner psyche? What does this foreshadow?
2. Curley's wife reveals much more about herself during the moments before her death. What do you think of the way the men treat her? Are they justified in treating her this way?
3. Discuss the significance of light-related imagery in these final sections in particular, as well as in the context of the entire book.
4. Do you think the death of Curley's wife comes as a surprise?
5. How does George react to the discovery of the body? How does this differ from Candy's reaction?
6. What is ironic about Lennie's hallucinations?
7. What do you think about the ending and Carlson's comment about George and Slim?
8. George's killing of Lennie mirrors what other event in this book? What does this signify?

Vocabulary (in order of appearance)

Part V:

- pulley: a wheel system used to transmit power
- slats: usually made out of wood or metal, a thin and flat strip of material
- sullen: resentful, sulking
- tenement: house used as a residence
- "pitcher": picture, i.e., Hollywood film
- earnest: very serious and honest in intention
- coarse: common; or harsh and rough in texture
- snivel: to cry or whine

Part VI:

- scud: to move or run quickly
- skitter: to move in a jittery manner
- gingham: a type of fabric for clothes
- woodenly: stiffly, lacking in emotion
- monotonous: tediously uniform in tone
- muzzle: the open end of a gun

Additional Homework

1. Arrange for a screening of the 1992 film adaptation of *Of Mice and Men*, starring Gary Sinise and John Malkovich. Alternatively, students can opt to watch the film on their own.

   Then, the students should write a five-paragraph essay that assesses the following:

   -What visual techniques are used to adapt the novel into movie format

   -How effective are such techniques?

   -What are the similarities and differences between Steinbeck's text and the movie adaption?

   Students should evaluate whether they believe the film adequate captures the tragedy of Steinbeck's work.
2. Research the title of the book, which is a reference to a poem by Robert Burns. What is the original context of the phrase? How is it related to the themes of the novella?

Day 5 - Discussion of Thought Questions

1. In the opening of Part V, Lennie speaks aloud to the dead puppy in the barn. What does this demonstrate about Lennie and his inner psyche? What does this foreshadow?

   Time: 10-15 minutes

   Discussion:

   In an unusual departure from the realistic starkness of the rest of the work, Lennie hallucinates in the final chapter, shortly before his death. These hallucinations are foreshadowed by his monologue directed at the dog. It seems that the threat of losing his dream to raise rabbits drives Lennie toward this level of self-delusion. In Part V, the "symptoms" are relatively mild--he is simply talking aloud to the dead dog.

   In Part VI, however, the threat to his dream is much more significant; Lennie is aware that he has done something irrevocably terrible that can destroy his dream. Thus, his "symptoms" are more serious; he actually hallucinates his Aunt Clara and a rabbit, but again, these hallucinations are manifested through his own speech.

2. Curley's wife reveals much more about herself during the moments before her death. What do you think of the way the men treat her? Are they justified in treating her this way?

   Time: 10 minutes

   Discussion:

   Curley's wife explicitly tells Lennie that she is extremely lonely, and she is not permitted to talk to anyone, which she finds unjust. "'Ain't I got a right to talk to nobody? Whatta they think I am, anyways?'"

   One might argue that this treatment on the part of the men is fair and safer for them. It is well known that Curley will be quick to start trouble with any man he suspects of consorting with his wife. As the son of the ranch boss, none of the workers want to incite his anger, start a brawl, or lose their jobs.

At the same time, the men are certainly quick to judge Curley's wife as a mere flirt and hussy. They do not consider her loneliness as the only woman among ranch workers, none of whom talk to her with respect and care. Thus, Curley's wife is another significant character who suffers from loneliness and unfulfilled dreams.

3. Discuss the significance of light-related imagery in these final sections in particular, as well as in the context of the entire book.

Time: 10 minutes

Discussion:

The novel opens with the fresh, light-filled description of the riverbank area that represents Lennie and George's safe haven. Light figures significantly throughout the rest of the novel. For example, the bunkhouse is always described as darker than the bright outdoors; the bunkhouse traps the men within their loneliness as ranch workers and stifles their dreams of better lives. Likewise, when the reader is first introduced to Curley's wife, she stands in the doorway and blocks the sunlight, foreshadowing the negative aspects of her presence.

In these final chapters, however, the sunlight is depicted as waning away. This reflects the culmination of the novel in tragedy: the manslaughter of Curley's wife, Lennie's death, the loss of George's dreams, and the end of their friendship. The lack of light is mentioned at points throughout Parts V and VI. In the opening of the final part, Steinbeck writes, "Already the sun had left the valley to go climbing up the slopes of the Gabilan mountains...." The sun is departing, leaving behind men without hope or dreams.

4. Do you think the death of Curley's wife comes as a surprise?

Time: 5 minutes

Discussion:

In short, certain details/events have been planted to lead up to the manslaughter of Curley's wife. First, the incident that forces George and Lennie to leave their former place of employment in Weed involves a young girl. An innocent act--Lennie touching her soft dress--leads to disaster. Lennie has proven that he doesn't understand social rules regarding the opposite sex, and that he tightens his grip when frightened.

Furthermore, it is known that Lennie has accidentally killed a mouse, then a puppy. His strength is evident in his crushing of Curley's fist. Each living creature that Lennie hurts grows larger: mouse, puppy, and then human.

5. How does George react to the discovery of the body? How does this differ from Candy's reaction?

Time: 5-10 minutes

Discussion:

In a clear indication of the depth of their friendship, George's foremost concern is Lennie's welfare. He wants to protect Lennie from the wrath of the other men, and he also realizes that Lennie will not be able to survive escaping on his own; he would starve to death. George then thinks ahead to how he can best protect Lennie from the probable lynch mob.

Candy, however, is more concerned with the loss of their dream. When George leaves (to steal Carlson's gun and feign shock at the death), Candy briefly reminisces the details of the unattainable dream, even shedding tears. Both men aptly realize that this event ruins any opportunity of them achieving their dream home. For George, his loss is greater because he will lose a dear friend and become one of the many anonymous, lonely migrant ranch workers.

6. What is ironic about Lennie's hallucinations?

Time: 5 minutes

Discussion: Hallucinations are associated with people who are not mentally stable or experiencing delusions. However, in his hallucinations of the rabbit and of Aunt Clara, Lennie finally seems to be much more perceptive than the simple-minded, childlike persona he displays previously in *Of Mice and Men*. He entertains real-life fears of being a burden upon George and being deserted by his friend because he causes too much trouble. He also recognizes that he will be unable to achieve his dream of raising rabbits.

7. What do you think about the ending and Carlson's comment about George and Slim?

Time: 5 minutes

Discussion: Only Slim fully understands the extent of George's grief and sorrow over the loss of his friend. The other men lack any human compassion. Carlson and Curley simply cannot comprehend why George would be upset that he has just killed his best friend. Carlson appears to be genuinely perplexed by George's profound sadness. This highlights how the ranch workers' loneliness and lifestyle have stripped them of any sense of compassion and care.

8. George's killing of Lennie mirrors what other event in this book? What does this signify?

Time: 5-10 minutes

Discussion:

Earlier in the novella, Carlson kills Candy's sick, old dog, and Candy later expresses regret for having not killed the dog himself and allowed a stranger to do it. Acting on the same sentiment, George takes agency over Lennie's fate. He knows that he is the only person who truly loves Lennie and will do him as much justice as possible, given the circumstances.

Unlike Candy, George refuses to stand by and let Lennie suffer at the hands of those who do not care for him. Thus, he kills Lennie himself--and in the process, also a part of his own human self. Without Lennie's friendship to differentiate him from others, George becomes fully immersed in a common life of loneliness and unfulfilled dreams, just like the other ranch workers.

Day 5 - Short Answer Quiz

1. On what day do the events of Parts V and VI take place?

_____

2. Why is Lennie so upset in the beginning of Part V?

_____

3. Where did Curley and his wife meet, and when did they get married?

_____

4. What does Curley's wife offer to Lennie, which results in her death?

_____

5. Who is first to discover the body of Curley's wife?

1) George

2) Curley

3) Slim

4) Candy

_____

6. What are two of George's concerns when he realizes that Lennie has accidentally killed Curley's wife?

7. About whom does Lennie hallucinate?

_____

8. The men assume that _____ has stolen Carlson's gun.

   1) Curley

   2) George

   3) Lennie

   4) Candy

_____

9. Why does Curley insist that George join the lynch mob?

_____

10. Where are George and Slim headed at the end of the novel?

_____

Short Answer Quiz Key

1. Sunday
2. He has killed the puppy accidentally, which he fears means that George will not let him raise rabbits.
3. At the Riverside Dance Palace, and they married the night that they met.
4. Curley's wife offers Lennie the opportunity to stroke her soft hair.
5. 4) Candy
6. 1) that Lennie will be hurt by the men

   2) that Lennie may starve to death on his own
7. Aunt Clara and a giant rabbit.
8. 3) Lennie
9. To prove that he has not had a hand in Lennie's escape or the death of Curley's wife
10. To go into to town to have a drink

Day 5 - Vocabulary Quiz

Terms	Answers
1. ____ The ____ system was used to transport the heavy blocks of concrete.	A. coarse
	B. monotonous
	C. wooden
	D. snivel
2. ____ After being punished, the student remained __ and silent.	E. sullen
	F. pulley
3. ____ Shocked by the tragedy, her movements were stiff and ___.	G. skittered
	H. muzzle
	I. tenement
	J. 'pitchers'
4. ____ She dressed up in a ruffled blouse and ___ skirt.	K. slats
	L. gingham
5. ____ Curley's wife imagined that she would someday star in ___.	M. scudded
	N. earnest
6. ____ The lecture was difficult to follow in part because the professor's voice was so ____.	
7. ____ The ceiling ____ allowed sunlight to stream through in between them.	
8. ____ The deer _____ away from the oncoming car.	
9. ____ Despite her lack of skill, the tennis instuctor was charmed by her ___ determination to improve her performance on the court.	

10. _____ After working the entire day, the ranch workers returned to the _____ to rest.
11. _____ He pointed the _____ of the gun at the target.
12. _____ The rabbit _____ away from the pursuing dogs.
13. _____ The child began to _____ at the thought of losing the toy.
14. _____ The texture of his beard was quite _____ and scratchy.

Vocabulary Quiz Answer Key

1. F
2. E
3. C
4. L
5. J
6. B
7. K
8. G
9. N
10. I
11. H
12. M
13. D
14. A

Day 5 - Classroom Activities

1. Classroom Debate

Kind of Activity: classrroom-wide
Objective: to thoughtfully and thoroughly evaluate ethical issues regarding manslaughter v. murder
Time: 40 minutes

Structure:

Divide the class into two groups.

+ One group will argue that George's killing of Lennie is justified.

+ The other group will argue that George's killing of Lennie is unjustified.

Students should compare George's killing of Lennie with Lennie's accidental killing of Curley's wife, as well.

For fifteen minutes, allow the students to discuss their argument amongst themselves. They should create a poster that outlines the main points of the argument, citing relevant examples from the text and from real life experiences. The students should also prepare a brief five-minute presentation for the class.

Allow each group to present the poster and explain the argument to the class.

Then, for the final fifteen minutes, instigate a class-wide discussion regarding the arguments presented by both sides. Is George's action kind or cruel? Is it just? Is it the same in nature as Lennie's manslaughter of Curley's wife? Is that indeed manslaughter, or is Lennie aware enough of the consequences of his action to have controlled himself?

Assessment Criteria:

+ that students work cooperatively with one another and proactively share opinions, offer personal experiences, etc.

+ that students critically evaluate these violent acts in the context of the entire novel

+ that students demonstrate strong speaking skills

+ that students develop a coherent argument in support of their opinions

+ that students are able to critically evaluate opposing peers' arguments and to respond appropriately

2. Mock Trial

Kind of Activity: class-wide
Objective: to present oral arguments to the class, accurately recalling in-text characterizations and events
Time: 45 minutes

Structure:

Divide the class into the following roles:

Lennie

Lennie's lawyer(s) (imagined character)

George

Slim

Candy

Crooks

Curley

Prosecutor(s) (imagined character)

The rest of the students should make up the trial jury.

Imagine that instead of this ending, Lennie is arrested by the proper authorities and put to trial for the death of Curley's wife.

In a trial setting, each character should be cross-examined by Lennie's lawyer(s) and the prosecutor(s) in order to evaluate his killing of Curley's wife. Students should accurately portray their characters' mindset and thoughts regarding Lennie.

Then, the prosecution and the defense will present their final arguments regarding Lennie's actions to the jury. The jury will then decide, based upon the trial proceedings, the appropriate punishment for Lennie: capital punishment, jail time, none, etc.

Assessment Criteria:

+ that students realistically dramatize their personas and articulate their thoughts clearly to the jury

+ that the prosecution and the defense make convincing and logical arguments to support their respective stances

+ that the jury assesses all testimony and arguments in a logical manner in order to come to a reasonable verdict

+ that all students demonstrate full understanding of the events of the text, but also of the contexts in which they occur and how such subtleties may impact their perceptions of Lennie and his actions

Final Paper

Essay Questions

1. The title of this novella is taken from the following excerpt of a Robert Burns poem:

   "The best laid schemes o' Mice an' Men,

   Gang aft agley,

   An' lea'e us nought but grief an' pain,

   For promis'd joy!"

   What do you think is the significance of this reference?

2. What is the significance of naming in Steinbeck's *Of Mice and Men*, with reference to characters in particular?

3. Originally, Steinbeck's work was meant to be named *Something That Happened*. Why?

4. How relevant do you think fate is in the events of *Of Mice and Men*?

5. On the whole, is Steinbeck's writing style more dramatic or descriptive in *Of Mice and Men*?

6. What is the greatest tragedy of *Of Mice and Men*? What do you think will become of George, now that Lennie is dead?

Advice on research sources

A. School or community library

Ask your reference librarian for help locating books on the following subjects:

* John Steinbeck and his literary generation

* *Of Mice and Men*

* The Great Depression

* migrant workers in California during the Great Depression

* film versions of *Of Mice and men* (1939 and 1992)

B. Personal experience

Have you ever been a victim of social equality, based on gender, race or religious belief, etc.? Have you ever thought about the importance of friendship, the impact of loneliness on a human? Have you ever encountered difficult conflict in a friendship, in which "doing right" by your friend could be construed as hurtful to your friend and to yourself?

Grading rubric for essays

Style:

* words: spelling and diction

* sentences: grammar and punctuation

* paragraphs: organization

* essay: structure

* argument: rhetoric, reasonableness, creativity

Content:

* accuracy

* use of evidence

* addresses the question

* completeness

* uses literary concepts

Advice on research sources

Final Paper Answer Key

Remember that essays about literature should not be graded with a cookie-cutter approach whereby specific words or ideas are required. See the grading rubric above for a variety of criteria to use in assessing answers to the essay questions. This answer key thus functions as a store of ideas for students who need additional guidance in framing their answers.

1. The title of this novella is taken from the following excerpt of a Robert Burns poem:

   "The best laid schemes o' Mice an' Men,

   Gang aft agley,

   An' lea'e us nought but grief an' pain,

   For promis'd joy!"

   What do you think is the significance of this reference?

   First, by comparing men with mice, this implies that humans--despite their increased levels of intelligence and autonomy over their lives--are no less in control of their fates than simple animals. This is reinforced by the rest of the quote, which generally means that no matter how planned one may be, such plans may easily be destroyed by uncontrollable circumstances.

   Students should relate this interpretation to the text. George, Lennie and then Candy develop a fairly concrete plan to achieve their dream of owning a piece of land together. However, seemingly unavoidable events converge to prevent them from achieving this dream. Lennie's strength is repeatedly displayed throughout the novel as an inadvertent source of conflict, from the incident in Weed to his accidental killing of small mice, and so on.

   Although the men anticipate "promis'd joy," in the end, George is left with nothing but "grief an' pain" as he confronts the lonely life of a friendless migrant ranch worker.

2. What is the significance of naming in Steinbeck's *Of Mice and Men*, with reference to characters in particular?

Naming, or the lack thereof, helps to exploit the features of certain characters. For example, Lennie's ironic last name - "Small" - highlights the very important characteristic that leads to his downfall. Furthermore, his unawareness of his own strength causes him to inadvertently kill Curley's wife, thus precipitating his own death.

Crooks is named for his crippled back. This simple nickname, based upon an external feature, demonstrates how others view him and allow their treatment of him to be influenced by their perception of his race and affliction.

Likewise, Candy is an unexpected name for a much older man who has lived a long and full life. This reflects how he is not taken seriously by his peers, which he complains about to George and Lennie. Because he is crippled and unable to work on the ranch like the others, he is disrespected and not regarded seriously.

Curley's wife (and the ranch boss) remain mysteriously unnamed throughout the entire novella. Again, this highlights the fact that she is disregarded as practically a non-entity by the male ranch workers. This contributes to her extreme loneliness and desperation for a better life.

A strong essay will hit upon some of the above examples from the text to support the student's argument.

3. Originally, Steinbeck's work was meant to be named *Something That Happened*. Why?

Given the gravity of the tragic events in *Of Mice and Men*, the original title seems fairly flippant, but this is perhaps Steinbeck's intention. He wishes to describe in poignant detail the loneliness, hardships, and general misery experienced by migrant ranch workers during the Great Depression in California. These men are unfamiliar with concepts of human compassion, warmth, and friendship. Thus, something even as terrible a man having to kill his best friend is simply "something that happened."

This nonchalant description calls attention to the indifference that develops among people who have suffered great hardships and have been lonely for all of their lives. Carlson conveys this aptly in his final lines of *Of Mice and Men* as well, when he demonstrates his lack of understanding for George's grief.

4. How relevant do you think fate is in the events of *Of Mice and Men*?

The structure of the novel, as well as Steinbeck's hints in each section, make Lennie's fate seem inevitable. We start out with reference to the incident in Weed, a clear foreshadowing of worse mishaps to come, and George is very insistent upon Lennie returning to the riverbank if anything goes wrong at their new job. This hints to the reader that something *will* go wrong.

This presentiment is reinforced by the knowledge of Lennie's dead mice. His unthinking strength is displayed in the fight against Curley, as well as the other men's repeated warnings against him not to kill his puppy. Inevitably, Lennie does kill his puppy.

Lennie himself, as well as George, also realizes that Curley's wife presents a danger to them. Although she has done nothing overtly wrong in the novel, their identification of her as a negative force compels the reader to guess that something bad will happen to the main two protagonists because of her, whether directly or indirectly.

The death of Candy's dog at the hands of Carlson also foreshadows how George will be fated to kill Lennie himself at the conclusion of the novel.

5. On the whole, is Steinbeck's writing style more dramatic or descriptive in *Of Mice and Men*?

As this text was originally intended to be a play, Steinbeck's novel seems more dramatic than descriptive. The descriptions that do occur are almost purely for settings, and as expected of a play script, are found at the beginning of each new section or "scene." Furthermore, he conveys most of the characters' features through their actions, always simple and direct, and their accurate dialogue, replete with colloquialisms and dialects. Taken together, this renders Steinbeck's text more dramatic than descriptive.

Good essays will note the original intent of the author to make this a screenplay, as well as its adaptability into other film versions and a successful stage play. Such essays will also include the details regarding how each section is like a "scene," including the stage description at the beginning of each so-called scene. The use of dialogue and character gesture to convey action and information will also be noted.

6. What is the greatest tragedy of *Of Mice and Men*? What do you think will become of George, now that Lennie is dead?

Ostensibly, the tragedy includes the deaths of both Curley's wife and of Lennie, particularly because George must make the extraordinarily difficult and painful decision to kill Lennie himself.

However, the true tragedy is the lack of fulfillment of dreams. This is particularly true in the case of George, who is much younger than Candy and has his whole life ahead of him. Throughout most of the novel, he distinguishes himself from the other ranch workers because of his closeness with Lennie and his secret dream, seemingly attainable, to own a piece of land in the future, so that he can be his own boss. Thus, George is not yet a victim of loneliness and unfulfilled dreams, two key themes in this novella. Then, with Lennie's death, George loses everything - he will end up just like the others. He must resign himself to a life common to most migrant ranch workers: lonely, unfulfilled, unhappy, lacking companionship and human warmth.

Final Exam

A. Multiple Choice

Circle the letter corresponding to the best answer.

   1. The title of this work is derived from:

      (A) Steinbeck's imagination.
      (B) a poem by Robert Burns
      (C) a film by the same name.
      (D) a play by the same name.

   2. Lennie and George were introduced through:

      (A) George's Aunt Clara
      (B) Lennie's Aunt Clara
      (C) George's parents
      (D) Lennie's parents

   3. George and Lennie earn money as:

      (A) migrant ranch workers
      (B) nothing--they are unemployed
      (C) swampers
      (D) cowboys

   4. The place by the river is NOT where:

      (A) George and Lennie spend the night before reporting to work.
      (B) Lennie retreats after killing Curley's wife.
      (C) George tells Lennie to go if something bad happens.
      (D) Carlson kills Candy's dog.

   5. Curley is the __ of the ranch boss.

      (A) nephew
      (B) cousin
      (C) son
      (D) brother

6. George feels all of the following toward Lennie at some point in the text, except for:

(A) exasperation and anger
(B) concern and love
(C) protectiveness
(D) hatred

7. Who kills Candy's dog?

(A) Slim
(B) Carlson
(C) George
(D) Lennie

8. In the second section, Slim possesses something that Lennie desires. What is it?

(A) a pulp magazine
(B) ketchup
(C) a Luger
(D) puppies

9. Slim is described as all of the following, except:

(A) having authority
(B) belligerent
(C) a good listener
(D) dignified

10. The men seem to treat Curley's wife poorly because:

(A) she is too successful
(B) she is a flirt
(C) she is unattractive
(D) she is African American

11. Crooks is the

    (A) gardener
    (B) stable buck
    (C) swamper
    (D) ranch boss

12. Who steals Carlson's Luger?

    (A) Slim
    (B) George
    (C) Lennie
    (D) Crooks

13. The mob led by Curley intend to do what to Lennie?

    (A) arrest him
    (B) beat him
    (C) kill him
    (D) help him to escape

14. All of the following themes are apparent in this novella, except:

    (A) unfulfilled dreams
    (B) social inequality
    (C) loneliness
    (D) transitioning from adolescence to adulthood

15. George's killing of Lennie is an act of:

    (A) compassionate premeditation
    (B) accident
    (C) malicious premeditaiton
    (D) inexplicable cruelty

B. Short Answer

1. What do Curley's wife and Crooks have in common?

_____

2. Who says: "Now what the hell ya suppose is eatin' them two guys?" When is this statement made, and whom does it describe?

_____

3. Briefly describe one thing per character listed below that the dream will provide:

Lennie

George

Candy

Crooks

_____

C. Vocabulary

Terms

1. _____ type of plant; Lennie wants to use it to feed rabbits
2. _____ nervous or alarmed by the future
3. _____ belligerent
4. _____ a top-security jail located in California
5. _____ a card game with multiple players
6. _____ to collect in increments, or gradually
7. _____ rough in texture
8. _____ demeaning in nature
9. _____ a bundle of clothes or bedding
10. _____ streaked with gray
11. _____ a bother or an annoyance
12. _____ distant; having the air of being removed or superior
13. _____ to assess
14. _____ gloomy or sullen
15. _____ very serious and honest in intention
16. _____ a type of fabric
17. _____ tediously uniform in tone
18. _____ nonsense
19. _____ feeling shame or disappointment

Answers

A. monotonous
B. apprehensive
C. morose
D. imperious
E. aloof
F. crestfallen
G. appraise
H. nuisance
I. tenement
J. San Quentin
K. alfalfa
L. grizzled
M. gingham
N. accumulate
O. baloney
P. earnest
Q. mottled
R. pugnacious
S. derogatory
T. bindle
U. euchre
V. coarse

20. _____ being
    arrogantly
    self-assured
21. _____ being marked
    by splotches of color
22. _____ dwelling
    where people reside

D. Short Essays

1. Who do you think is the most sympathetic character in *Of Mice and Men*, and why?

_____

_____

_____

_____

2. Although Lennie and George certainly share a close friendship, they do experience conflict as well. Describe three such conflicts.

_____

_____

_____

_____

3. Discuss the significance of light in *Of Mice and Men.*

_____

_____

_____

_____

Final Exam Answer Key

A. Multiple Choice Answer Key

1. B
2. B
3. A
4. D
5. C
6. D
7. B
8. D
9. B
10. B
11. B
12. B
13. C
14. D
15. A

B. Short Answer Key

1. They are both lonely and ostracized by the male ranch workers.
2. Slim says the statement at the very end of the novel, after George has killed Lennie. He is referring to George and Slim.
3. Lennie: raising rabbits

   George: independence, ownership of land

   Candy: respect and dignity (instead of being treated like a cripple at the ranch)

   Crooks: companionship

C. Vocabulary Answer Key

1. K
2. B
3. R
4. J
5. U
6. N
7. V
8. S
9. T
10. L
11. H
12. E
13. G
14. C
15. P
16. M
17. A
18. O
19. F
20. D
21. Q
22. I

D. Short Essays Answer Key

1. Answers will vary, depending on the student's selection. Students should simply demonstrate clear knowledge of the character, his or her actions in the book, and why the character's internal features and actions make him/her a sympathetic figure.
2. Students should mention some of the following incidents:

   Lennie forgets to obey George about not speaking to anyone.

   Lennie's childlike simplicity, like his desire for ketchup with his can of beans, sometimes frustrates George.

   Lennie's killing of Curley's wife causes George to have to kill him as well.

   Lennie tells Crooks about their dream, against George's explicit instructions.

George does not allow Lennie to keep the dead mouse in his pocket.

3. Light figures prominently in this short work as an indicator of events that will occur and where they occur. The book opens with hope, particularly because George and Lennie are in their sunlight-filled haven by the river. The bunkhouse is described as a dark place, just like Crooks's room with its "meager yellow light," signifying his unhappy life of loneliness. In the final two sections, preceding the events that lead to Lennie's death at George's hand, the sun is descending because it is late afternoon. Thus, light reflects the tone of the novella's events.